BIG PRINT
Address Book

NAME

ADDRESS

HOME

MOBILE

WORK / FAX

E-MAIL

BIRTHDAY, ANNIVERSARY ETC

NAME

ADDRESS

HOME

MOBILE

WORK / FAX

E-MAIL

BIRTHDAY, ANNIVERSARY ETC

NAME

ADDRESS

HOME

MOBILE

WORK / FAX

E-MAIL

BIRTHDAY, ANNIVERSARY ETC

NAME

Address

Home

Mobile

Work / Fax

E-Mail

Birthday, Anniversary etc

NAME

Address

Home

Mobile

Work / Fax

E-Mail

Birthday, Anniversary etc

NAME

Address

Home

Mobile

Work / Fax

E-Mail

Birthday, Anniversary etc

NAME

Address

Home

Mobile

Work / Fax

E-Mail

Birthday, Anniversary etc

NAME

Address

Home

Mobile

Work / Fax

E-Mail

Birthday, Anniversary etc

NAME

Address

Home

Mobile

Work / Fax

E-Mail

Birthday, Anniversary etc

NAME

ADDRESS

HOME

MOBILE

WORK / FAX

E-MAIL

BIRTHDAY, ANNIVERSARY ETC

NAME

ADDRESS

HOME

MOBILE

WORK / FAX

E-MAIL

BIRTHDAY, ANNIVERSARY ETC

NAME

ADDRESS

HOME

MOBILE

WORK / FAX

E-MAIL

BIRTHDAY, ANNIVERSARY ETC

NAME

ADDRESS

HOME

MOBILE

WORK / FAX

E-MAIL

BIRTHDAY, ANNIVERSARY ETC

NAME

ADDRESS

HOME

MOBILE

WORK / FAX

E-MAIL

BIRTHDAY, ANNIVERSARY ETC

NAME

ADDRESS

HOME

MOBILE

WORK / FAX

E-MAIL

BIRTHDAY, ANNIVERSARY ETC

NAME

ADDRESS

HOME

MOBILE

WORK / FAX

E-MAIL

BIRTHDAY, ANNIVERSARY ETC

NAME

ADDRESS

HOME

MOBILE

WORK / FAX

E-MAIL

BIRTHDAY, ANNIVERSARY ETC

NAME

ADDRESS

HOME

MOBILE

WORK / FAX

E-MAIL

BIRTHDAY, ANNIVERSARY ETC

NAME

ADDRESS

HOME

MOBILE

WORK / FAX

E-MAIL

BIRTHDAY, ANNIVERSARY ETC

NAME

ADDRESS

HOME

MOBILE

WORK / FAX

E-MAIL

BIRTHDAY, ANNIVERSARY ETC

NAME

ADDRESS

HOME

MOBILE

WORK / FAX

E-MAIL

BIRTHDAY, ANNIVERSARY ETC

NAME

Address

Home

Mobile

Work / Fax

E-Mail

Birthday, Anniversary etc

NAME

Address

Home

Mobile

Work / Fax

E-Mail

Birthday, Anniversary etc

NAME

Address

Home

Mobile

Work / Fax

E-Mail

Birthday, Anniversary etc

NAME

Address

Home

Mobile

Work / Fax

E-Mail

Birthday, Anniversary etc

NAME

Address

Home

Mobile

Work / Fax

E-Mail

Birthday, Anniversary etc

NAME

Address

Home

Mobile

Work / Fax

E-Mail

Birthday, Anniversary etc

NAME

ADDRESS

HOME

MOBILE

WORK / FAX

E-MAIL

BIRTHDAY, ANNIVERSARY ETC

NAME

ADDRESS

HOME

MOBILE

WORK / FAX

E-MAIL

BIRTHDAY, ANNIVERSARY ETC

NAME

ADDRESS

HOME

MOBILE

WORK / FAX

E-MAIL

BIRTHDAY, ANNIVERSARY ETC

NAME

Address

Home

Mobile

Work / Fax

E-Mail

Birthday, Anniversary etc

NAME

Address

Home

Mobile

Work / Fax

E-Mail

Birthday, Anniversary etc

NAME

Address

Home

Mobile

Work / Fax

E-Mail

Birthday, Anniversary etc

NAME

ADDRESS

HOME

MOBILE

WORK / FAX

E-MAIL

BIRTHDAY, ANNIVERSARY ETC

NAME

ADDRESS

HOME

MOBILE

WORK / FAX

E-MAIL

BIRTHDAY, ANNIVERSARY ETC

NAME

ADDRESS

HOME

MOBILE

WORK / FAX

E-MAIL

BIRTHDAY, ANNIVERSARY ETC

NAME

ADDRESS

HOME

MOBILE

WORK / FAX

E-MAIL

BIRTHDAY, ANNIVERSARY ETC

NAME

ADDRESS

HOME

MOBILE

WORK / FAX

E-MAIL

BIRTHDAY, ANNIVERSARY ETC

NAME

ADDRESS

HOME

MOBILE

WORK / FAX

E-MAIL

BIRTHDAY, ANNIVERSARY ETC

NAME

Address

Home

Mobile

Work / Fax

E-Mail

Birthday, Anniversary etc

NAME

Address

Home

Mobile

Work / Fax

E-Mail

Birthday, Anniversary etc

NAME

Address

Home

Mobile

Work / Fax

E-Mail

Birthday, Anniversary etc

NAME

ADDRESS

HOME

MOBILE

WORK / FAX

E-MAIL

BIRTHDAY, ANNIVERSARY ETC

NAME

ADDRESS

HOME

MOBILE

WORK / FAX

E-MAIL

BIRTHDAY, ANNIVERSARY ETC

NAME

ADDRESS

HOME

MOBILE

WORK / FAX

E-MAIL

BIRTHDAY, ANNIVERSARY ETC

NAME

ADDRESS

HOME

MOBILE

WORK / FAX

E-MAIL

BIRTHDAY, ANNIVERSARY ETC

NAME

ADDRESS

HOME

MOBILE

WORK / FAX

E-MAIL

BIRTHDAY, ANNIVERSARY ETC

NAME

ADDRESS

HOME

MOBILE

WORK / FAX

E-MAIL

BIRTHDAY, ANNIVERSARY ETC

NAME

ADDRESS

HOME

MOBILE

WORK / FAX

E-MAIL

BIRTHDAY, ANNIVERSARY ETC

NAME

ADDRESS

HOME

MOBILE

WORK / FAX

E-MAIL

BIRTHDAY, ANNIVERSARY ETC

NAME

ADDRESS

HOME

MOBILE

WORK / FAX

E-MAIL

BIRTHDAY, ANNIVERSARY ETC

NAME

ADDRESS

HOME

MOBILE

WORK / FAX

E-MAIL

BIRTHDAY, ANNIVERSARY ETC

NAME

ADDRESS

HOME

MOBILE

WORK / FAX

E-MAIL

BIRTHDAY, ANNIVERSARY ETC

NAME

ADDRESS

HOME

MOBILE

WORK / FAX

E-MAIL

BIRTHDAY, ANNIVERSARY ETC

NAME

Address

Home

Mobile

Work / Fax

E-Mail

Birthday, Anniversary etc

NAME

Address

Home

Mobile

Work / Fax

E-Mail

Birthday, Anniversary etc

NAME

Address

Home

Mobile

Work / Fax

E-Mail

Birthday, Anniversary etc

NAME

ADDRESS

HOME

MOBILE

WORK / FAX

E-MAIL

BIRTHDAY, ANNIVERSARY ETC

NAME

ADDRESS

HOME

MOBILE

WORK / FAX

E-MAIL

BIRTHDAY, ANNIVERSARY ETC

NAME

ADDRESS

HOME

MOBILE

WORK / FAX

E-MAIL

BIRTHDAY, ANNIVERSARY ETC

NAME

Address

Home

Mobile

Work / Fax

E-Mail

Birthday, Anniversary etc

NAME

Address

Home

Mobile

Work / Fax

E-Mail

Birthday, Anniversary etc

NAME

Address

Home

Mobile

Work / Fax

E-Mail

Birthday, Anniversary etc

NAME

ADDRESS

HOME

MOBILE

WORK / FAX

E-MAIL

BIRTHDAY, ANNIVERSARY ETC

NAME

ADDRESS

HOME

MOBILE

WORK / FAX

E-MAIL

BIRTHDAY, ANNIVERSARY ETC

NAME

ADDRESS

HOME

MOBILE

WORK / FAX

E-MAIL

BIRTHDAY, ANNIVERSARY ETC

NAME

ADDRESS

HOME

MOBILE

WORK / FAX

E-MAIL

BIRTHDAY, ANNIVERSARY ETC

NAME

ADDRESS

HOME

MOBILE

WORK / FAX

E-MAIL

BIRTHDAY, ANNIVERSARY ETC

NAME

ADDRESS

HOME

MOBILE

WORK / FAX

E-MAIL

BIRTHDAY, ANNIVERSARY ETC

NAME

Address

Home

Mobile

Work / Fax

E-Mail

Birthday, Anniversary etc

NAME

Address

Home

Mobile

Work / Fax

E-Mail

Birthday, Anniversary etc

NAME

Address

Home

Mobile

Work / Fax

E-Mail

Birthday, Anniversary etc

NAME

ADDRESS

HOME

MOBILE

WORK / FAX

E-MAIL

BIRTHDAY, ANNIVERSARY ETC

NAME

ADDRESS

HOME

MOBILE

WORK / FAX

E-MAIL

BIRTHDAY, ANNIVERSARY ETC

NAME

ADDRESS

HOME

MOBILE

WORK / FAX

E-MAIL

BIRTHDAY, ANNIVERSARY ETC

NAME

Address

Home

Mobile

Work / Fax

E-Mail

Birthday, Anniversary etc

NAME

Address

Home

Mobile

Work / Fax

E-Mail

Birthday, Anniversary etc

NAME

Address

Home

Mobile

Work / Fax

E-Mail

Birthday, Anniversary etc

NAME

Address

Home

Mobile

Work / Fax

E-Mail

Birthday, Anniversary etc

NAME

Address

Home

Mobile

Work / Fax

E-Mail

Birthday, Anniversary etc

NAME

Address

Home

Mobile

Work / Fax

E-Mail

Birthday, Anniversary etc

NAME

ADDRESS

HOME

MOBILE

WORK / FAX

E-MAIL

BIRTHDAY, ANNIVERSARY ETC

NAME

ADDRESS

HOME

MOBILE

WORK / FAX

E-MAIL

BIRTHDAY, ANNIVERSARY ETC

NAME

ADDRESS

HOME

MOBILE

WORK / FAX

E-MAIL

BIRTHDAY, ANNIVERSARY ETC

NAME

ADDRESS

HOME

MOBILE

WORK / FAX

E-MAIL

BIRTHDAY, ANNIVERSARY ETC

NAME

ADDRESS

HOME

MOBILE

WORK / FAX

E-MAIL

BIRTHDAY, ANNIVERSARY ETC

NAME

ADDRESS

HOME

MOBILE

WORK / FAX

E-MAIL

BIRTHDAY, ANNIVERSARY ETC

NAME

ADDRESS

HOME

MOBILE

WORK / FAX

E-MAIL

BIRTHDAY, ANNIVERSARY ETC

NAME

ADDRESS

HOME

MOBILE

WORK / FAX

E-MAIL

BIRTHDAY, ANNIVERSARY ETC

NAME

ADDRESS

HOME

MOBILE

WORK / FAX

E-MAIL

BIRTHDAY, ANNIVERSARY ETC

NAME

ADDRESS

HOME

MOBILE

WORK / FAX

E-MAIL

BIRTHDAY, ANNIVERSARY ETC

NAME

ADDRESS

HOME

MOBILE

WORK / FAX

E-MAIL

BIRTHDAY, ANNIVERSARY ETC

NAME

ADDRESS

HOME

MOBILE

WORK / FAX

E-MAIL

BIRTHDAY, ANNIVERSARY ETC

NAME

ADDRESS

HOME

MOBILE

WORK / FAX

E-MAIL

BIRTHDAY, ANNIVERSARY ETC

NAME

ADDRESS

HOME

MOBILE

WORK / FAX

E-MAIL

BIRTHDAY, ANNIVERSARY ETC

NAME

ADDRESS

HOME

MOBILE

WORK / FAX

E-MAIL

BIRTHDAY, ANNIVERSARY ETC

NAME

ADDRESS

HOME

MOBILE

WORK / FAX

E-MAIL

BIRTHDAY, ANNIVERSARY ETC

NAME

ADDRESS

HOME

MOBILE

WORK / FAX

E-MAIL

BIRTHDAY, ANNIVERSARY ETC

NAME

ADDRESS

HOME

MOBILE

WORK / FAX

E-MAIL

BIRTHDAY, ANNIVERSARY ETC

NAME

ADDRESS

HOME

MOBILE

WORK / FAX

E-MAIL

BIRTHDAY, ANNIVERSARY ETC

NAME

ADDRESS

HOME

MOBILE

WORK / FAX

E-MAIL

BIRTHDAY, ANNIVERSARY ETC

NAME

ADDRESS

HOME

MOBILE

WORK / FAX

E-MAIL

BIRTHDAY, ANNIVERSARY ETC

NAME

ADDRESS

HOME

MOBILE

WORK / FAX

E-MAIL

BIRTHDAY, ANNIVERSARY ETC

NAME

ADDRESS

HOME

MOBILE

WORK / FAX

E-MAIL

BIRTHDAY, ANNIVERSARY ETC

NAME

ADDRESS

HOME

MOBILE

WORK / FAX

E-MAIL

BIRTHDAY, ANNIVERSARY ETC

NAME

ADDRESS

HOME

MOBILE

WORK / FAX

E-MAIL

BIRTHDAY, ANNIVERSARY ETC

NAME

ADDRESS

HOME

MOBILE

WORK / FAX

E-MAIL

BIRTHDAY, ANNIVERSARY ETC

NAME

ADDRESS

HOME

MOBILE

WORK / FAX

E-MAIL

BIRTHDAY, ANNIVERSARY ETC

NAME

ADDRESS

HOME

MOBILE

WORK / FAX

E-MAIL

BIRTHDAY, ANNIVERSARY ETC

NAME

ADDRESS

HOME

MOBILE

WORK / FAX

E-MAIL

BIRTHDAY, ANNIVERSARY ETC

NAME

ADDRESS

HOME

MOBILE

WORK / FAX

E-MAIL

BIRTHDAY, ANNIVERSARY ETC

NAME

ADDRESS

HOME

MOBILE

WORK / FAX

E-MAIL

BIRTHDAY, ANNIVERSARY ETC

NAME

ADDRESS

HOME

MOBILE

WORK / FAX

E-MAIL

BIRTHDAY, ANNIVERSARY ETC

NAME

ADDRESS

HOME

MOBILE

WORK / FAX

E-MAIL

BIRTHDAY, ANNIVERSARY ETC

NAME

ADDRESS

HOME

MOBILE

WORK / FAX

E-MAIL

BIRTHDAY, ANNIVERSARY ETC

NAME

ADDRESS

HOME

MOBILE

WORK / FAX

E-MAIL

BIRTHDAY, ANNIVERSARY ETC

NAME

ADDRESS

HOME

MOBILE

WORK / FAX

E-MAIL

BIRTHDAY, ANNIVERSARY ETC

NAME

ADDRESS

HOME

MOBILE

WORK / FAX

E-MAIL

BIRTHDAY, ANNIVERSARY ETC

NAME

ADDRESS

HOME

MOBILE

WORK / FAX

E-MAIL

BIRTHDAY, ANNIVERSARY ETC

NAME

ADDRESS

HOME

MOBILE

WORK / FAX

E-MAIL

BIRTHDAY, ANNIVERSARY ETC

NAME

Address

Home

Mobile

Work / Fax

E-Mail

Birthday, Anniversary etc

NAME

Address

Home

Mobile

Work / Fax

E-Mail

Birthday, Anniversary etc

NAME

Address

Home

Mobile

Work / Fax

E-Mail

Birthday, Anniversary etc

NAME

ADDRESS

HOME

MOBILE

WORK / FAX

E-MAIL

BIRTHDAY, ANNIVERSARY ETC

NAME

ADDRESS

HOME

MOBILE

WORK / FAX

E-MAIL

BIRTHDAY, ANNIVERSARY ETC

NAME

ADDRESS

HOME

MOBILE

WORK / FAX

E-MAIL

BIRTHDAY, ANNIVERSARY ETC

NAME

ADDRESS

HOME

MOBILE

WORK / FAX

E-MAIL

BIRTHDAY, ANNIVERSARY ETC

NAME

ADDRESS

HOME

MOBILE

WORK / FAX

E-MAIL

BIRTHDAY, ANNIVERSARY ETC

NAME

ADDRESS

HOME

MOBILE

WORK / FAX

E-MAIL

BIRTHDAY, ANNIVERSARY ETC

NAME

ADDRESS

HOME

MOBILE

WORK / FAX

E-MAIL

BIRTHDAY, ANNIVERSARY ETC

NAME

ADDRESS

HOME

MOBILE

WORK / FAX

E-MAIL

BIRTHDAY, ANNIVERSARY ETC

NAME

ADDRESS

HOME

MOBILE

WORK / FAX

E-MAIL

BIRTHDAY, ANNIVERSARY ETC

NAME

ADDRESS

HOME

MOBILE

WORK / FAX

E-MAIL

BIRTHDAY, ANNIVERSARY ETC

NAME

ADDRESS

HOME

MOBILE

WORK / FAX

E-MAIL

BIRTHDAY, ANNIVERSARY ETC

NAME

ADDRESS

HOME

MOBILE

WORK / FAX

E-MAIL

BIRTHDAY, ANNIVERSARY ETC

NAME

ADDRESS

HOME

MOBILE

WORK / FAX

E-MAIL

BIRTHDAY, ANNIVERSARY ETC

NAME

ADDRESS

HOME

MOBILE

WORK / FAX

E-MAIL

BIRTHDAY, ANNIVERSARY ETC

NAME

ADDRESS

HOME

MOBILE

WORK / FAX

E-MAIL

BIRTHDAY, ANNIVERSARY ETC

NAME

ADDRESS

HOME

MOBILE

WORK / FAX

E-MAIL

BIRTHDAY, ANNIVERSARY ETC

NAME

ADDRESS

HOME

MOBILE

WORK / FAX

E-MAIL

BIRTHDAY, ANNIVERSARY ETC

NAME

ADDRESS

HOME

MOBILE

WORK / FAX

E-MAIL

BIRTHDAY, ANNIVERSARY ETC

NAME

ADDRESS

HOME

MOBILE

WORK / FAX

E-MAIL

BIRTHDAY, ANNIVERSARY ETC

NAME

ADDRESS

HOME

MOBILE

WORK / FAX

E-MAIL

BIRTHDAY, ANNIVERSARY ETC

NAME

ADDRESS

HOME

MOBILE

WORK / FAX

E-MAIL

BIRTHDAY, ANNIVERSARY ETC

NAME

ADDRESS

HOME

MOBILE

WORK / FAX

E-MAIL

BIRTHDAY, ANNIVERSARY ETC

NAME

ADDRESS

HOME

MOBILE

WORK / FAX

E-MAIL

BIRTHDAY, ANNIVERSARY ETC

NAME

ADDRESS

HOME

MOBILE

WORK / FAX

E-MAIL

BIRTHDAY, ANNIVERSARY ETC

NAME

Address

Home

Mobile

Work / Fax

E-Mail

Birthday, Anniversary etc

NAME

Address

Home

Mobile

Work / Fax

E-Mail

Birthday, Anniversary etc

NAME

Address

Home

Mobile

Work / Fax

E-Mail

Birthday, Anniversary etc

NAME

ADDRESS

HOME

MOBILE

WORK / FAX

E-MAIL

BIRTHDAY, ANNIVERSARY ETC

NAME

ADDRESS

HOME

MOBILE

WORK / FAX

E-MAIL

BIRTHDAY, ANNIVERSARY ETC

NAME

ADDRESS

HOME

MOBILE

WORK / FAX

E-MAIL

BIRTHDAY, ANNIVERSARY ETC

NAME

Address

Home

Mobile

Work / Fax

E-Mail

Birthday, Anniversary etc

NAME

Address

Home

Mobile

Work / Fax

E-Mail

Birthday, Anniversary etc

NAME

Address

Home

Mobile

Work / Fax

E-Mail

Birthday, Anniversary etc

NAME

ADDRESS

HOME

MOBILE

WORK / FAX

E-MAIL

BIRTHDAY, ANNIVERSARY ETC

NAME

ADDRESS

HOME

MOBILE

WORK / FAX

E-MAIL

BIRTHDAY, ANNIVERSARY ETC

NAME

ADDRESS

HOME

MOBILE

WORK / FAX

E-MAIL

BIRTHDAY, ANNIVERSARY ETC

NAME

ADDRESS

HOME

MOBILE

WORK / FAX

E-MAIL

BIRTHDAY, ANNIVERSARY ETC

NAME

ADDRESS

HOME

MOBILE

WORK / FAX

E-MAIL

BIRTHDAY, ANNIVERSARY ETC

NAME

ADDRESS

HOME

MOBILE

WORK / FAX

E-MAIL

BIRTHDAY, ANNIVERSARY ETC

NAME

Address

Home

Mobile

Work / Fax

E-Mail

Birthday, Anniversary etc

NAME

Address

Home

Mobile

Work / Fax

E-Mail

Birthday, Anniversary etc

NAME

Address

Home

Mobile

Work / Fax

E-Mail

Birthday, Anniversary etc

NAME

ADDRESS

HOME

MOBILE

WORK / FAX

E-MAIL

BIRTHDAY, ANNIVERSARY ETC

NAME

ADDRESS

HOME

MOBILE

WORK / FAX

E-MAIL

BIRTHDAY, ANNIVERSARY ETC

NAME

ADDRESS

HOME

MOBILE

WORK / FAX

E-MAIL

BIRTHDAY, ANNIVERSARY ETC

NAME

ADDRESS

HOME

MOBILE

WORK / FAX

E-MAIL

BIRTHDAY, ANNIVERSARY ETC

NAME

ADDRESS

HOME

MOBILE

WORK / FAX

E-MAIL

BIRTHDAY, ANNIVERSARY ETC

NAME

ADDRESS

HOME

MOBILE

WORK / FAX

E-MAIL

BIRTHDAY, ANNIVERSARY ETC

NAME

ADDRESS

HOME

MOBILE

WORK / FAX

E-MAIL

BIRTHDAY, ANNIVERSARY ETC

NAME

ADDRESS

HOME

MOBILE

WORK / FAX

E-MAIL

BIRTHDAY, ANNIVERSARY ETC

NAME

ADDRESS

HOME

MOBILE

WORK / FAX

E-MAIL

BIRTHDAY, ANNIVERSARY ETC

NAME

ADDRESS

HOME

MOBILE

WORK / FAX

E-MAIL

BIRTHDAY, ANNIVERSARY ETC

NAME

ADDRESS

HOME

MOBILE

WORK / FAX

E-MAIL

BIRTHDAY, ANNIVERSARY ETC

NAME

ADDRESS

HOME

MOBILE

WORK / FAX

E-MAIL

BIRTHDAY, ANNIVERSARY ETC

NAME

ADDRESS

HOME

MOBILE

WORK / FAX

E-MAIL

BIRTHDAY, ANNIVERSARY ETC

NAME

ADDRESS

HOME

MOBILE

WORK / FAX

E-MAIL

BIRTHDAY, ANNIVERSARY ETC

NAME

ADDRESS

HOME

MOBILE

WORK / FAX

E-MAIL

BIRTHDAY, ANNIVERSARY ETC

NAME

ADDRESS

HOME

MOBILE

WORK / FAX

E-MAIL

BIRTHDAY, ANNIVERSARY ETC

NAME

ADDRESS

HOME

MOBILE

WORK / FAX

E-MAIL

BIRTHDAY, ANNIVERSARY ETC

NAME

ADDRESS

HOME

MOBILE

WORK / FAX

E-MAIL

BIRTHDAY, ANNIVERSARY ETC

NAME

Address

Home

Mobile

Work / Fax

E-Mail

Birthday, Anniversary etc

NAME

Address

Home

Mobile

Work / Fax

E-Mail

Birthday, Anniversary etc

NAME

Address

Home

Mobile

Work / Fax

E-Mail

Birthday, Anniversary etc

NAME

ADDRESS

HOME

MOBILE

WORK / FAX

E-MAIL

BIRTHDAY, ANNIVERSARY ETC

NAME

ADDRESS

HOME

MOBILE

WORK / FAX

E-MAIL

BIRTHDAY, ANNIVERSARY ETC

NAME

ADDRESS

HOME

MOBILE

WORK / FAX

E-MAIL

BIRTHDAY, ANNIVERSARY ETC

NAME

ADDRESS

HOME

MOBILE

WORK / FAX

E-MAIL

BIRTHDAY, ANNIVERSARY ETC

NAME

ADDRESS

HOME

MOBILE

WORK / FAX

E-MAIL

BIRTHDAY, ANNIVERSARY ETC

NAME

ADDRESS

HOME

MOBILE

WORK / FAX

E-MAIL

BIRTHDAY, ANNIVERSARY ETC

NAME

ADDRESS

HOME

MOBILE

WORK / FAX

E-MAIL

BIRTHDAY, ANNIVERSARY ETC

NAME

ADDRESS

HOME

MOBILE

WORK / FAX

E-MAIL

BIRTHDAY, ANNIVERSARY ETC

NAME

ADDRESS

HOME

MOBILE

WORK / FAX

E-MAIL

BIRTHDAY, ANNIVERSARY ETC

NAME

ADDRESS

HOME

MOBILE

WORK / FAX

E-MAIL

BIRTHDAY, ANNIVERSARY ETC

NAME

ADDRESS

HOME

MOBILE

WORK / FAX

E-MAIL

BIRTHDAY, ANNIVERSARY ETC

NAME

ADDRESS

HOME

MOBILE

WORK / FAX

E-MAIL

BIRTHDAY, ANNIVERSARY ETC

NAME

ADDRESS

HOME

MOBILE

WORK / FAX

E-MAIL

BIRTHDAY, ANNIVERSARY ETC

NAME

ADDRESS

HOME

MOBILE

WORK / FAX

E-MAIL

BIRTHDAY, ANNIVERSARY ETC

NAME

ADDRESS

HOME

MOBILE

WORK / FAX

E-MAIL

BIRTHDAY, ANNIVERSARY ETC

NAME

ADDRESS

HOME

MOBILE

WORK / FAX

E-MAIL

BIRTHDAY, ANNIVERSARY ETC

NAME

ADDRESS

HOME

MOBILE

WORK / FAX

E-MAIL

BIRTHDAY, ANNIVERSARY ETC

NAME

ADDRESS

HOME

MOBILE

WORK / FAX

E-MAIL

BIRTHDAY, ANNIVERSARY ETC

NAME

ADDRESS

HOME

MOBILE

WORK / FAX

E-MAIL

BIRTHDAY, ANNIVERSARY ETC

NAME

ADDRESS

HOME

MOBILE

WORK / FAX

E-MAIL

BIRTHDAY, ANNIVERSARY ETC

NAME

ADDRESS

HOME

MOBILE

WORK / FAX

E-MAIL

BIRTHDAY, ANNIVERSARY ETC

NAME

ADDRESS

HOME

MOBILE

WORK / FAX

E-MAIL

BIRTHDAY, ANNIVERSARY ETC

NAME

ADDRESS

HOME

MOBILE

WORK / FAX

E-MAIL

BIRTHDAY, ANNIVERSARY ETC

NAME

ADDRESS

HOME

MOBILE

WORK / FAX

E-MAIL

BIRTHDAY, ANNIVERSARY ETC

NAME

Address

Home

Mobile

Work / Fax

E-Mail

Birthday, Anniversary etc

NAME

Address

Home

Mobile

Work / Fax

E-Mail

Birthday, Anniversary etc

NAME

Address

Home

Mobile

Work / Fax

E-Mail

Birthday, Anniversary etc

NAME

ADDRESS

HOME

MOBILE

WORK / FAX

E-MAIL

BIRTHDAY, ANNIVERSARY ETC

NAME

ADDRESS

HOME

MOBILE

WORK / FAX

E-MAIL

BIRTHDAY, ANNIVERSARY ETC

NAME

ADDRESS

HOME

MOBILE

WORK / FAX

E-MAIL

BIRTHDAY, ANNIVERSARY ETC

NAME

ADDRESS

HOME

MOBILE

WORK / FAX

E-MAIL

BIRTHDAY, ANNIVERSARY ETC

NAME

ADDRESS

HOME

MOBILE

WORK / FAX

E-MAIL

BIRTHDAY, ANNIVERSARY ETC

NAME

ADDRESS

HOME

MOBILE

WORK / FAX

E-MAIL

BIRTHDAY, ANNIVERSARY ETC

NAME

ADDRESS

HOME

MOBILE

WORK / FAX

E-MAIL

BIRTHDAY, ANNIVERSARY ETC

NAME

ADDRESS

HOME

MOBILE

WORK / FAX

E-MAIL

BIRTHDAY, ANNIVERSARY ETC

NAME

ADDRESS

HOME

MOBILE

WORK / FAX

E-MAIL

BIRTHDAY, ANNIVERSARY ETC

NAME

ADDRESS

HOME

MOBILE

WORK / FAX

E-MAIL

BIRTHDAY, ANNIVERSARY ETC

NAME

ADDRESS

HOME

MOBILE

WORK / FAX

E-MAIL

BIRTHDAY, ANNIVERSARY ETC

NAME

ADDRESS

HOME

MOBILE

WORK / FAX

E-MAIL

BIRTHDAY, ANNIVERSARY ETC

NAME

ADDRESS

HOME

MOBILE

WORK / FAX

E-MAIL

BIRTHDAY, ANNIVERSARY ETC

NAME

ADDRESS

HOME

MOBILE

WORK / FAX

E-MAIL

BIRTHDAY, ANNIVERSARY ETC

NAME

ADDRESS

HOME

MOBILE

WORK / FAX

E-MAIL

BIRTHDAY, ANNIVERSARY ETC

NAME

Address

Home

Mobile

Work / Fax

E-Mail

Birthday, Anniversary etc

NAME

Address

Home

Mobile

Work / Fax

E-Mail

Birthday, Anniversary etc

NAME

Address

Home

Mobile

Work / Fax

E-Mail

Birthday, Anniversary etc

NAME

ADDRESS

HOME

MOBILE

WORK / FAX

E-MAIL

BIRTHDAY, ANNIVERSARY ETC

NAME

ADDRESS

HOME

MOBILE

WORK / FAX

E-MAIL

BIRTHDAY, ANNIVERSARY ETC

NAME

ADDRESS

HOME

MOBILE

WORK / FAX

E-MAIL

BIRTHDAY, ANNIVERSARY ETC

NAME

ADDRESS

HOME

MOBILE

WORK / FAX

E-MAIL

BIRTHDAY, ANNIVERSARY ETC

NAME

ADDRESS

HOME

MOBILE

WORK / FAX

E-MAIL

BIRTHDAY, ANNIVERSARY ETC

NAME

ADDRESS

HOME

MOBILE

WORK / FAX

E-MAIL

BIRTHDAY, ANNIVERSARY ETC

NAME

Address

Home

Mobile

Work / Fax

E-Mail

Birthday, Anniversary etc

NAME

Address

Home

Mobile

Work / Fax

E-Mail

Birthday, Anniversary etc

NAME

Address

Home

Mobile

Work / Fax

E-Mail

Birthday, Anniversary etc

NAME

ADDRESS

HOME

MOBILE

WORK / FAX

E-MAIL

BIRTHDAY, ANNIVERSARY ETC

NAME

ADDRESS

HOME

MOBILE

WORK / FAX

E-MAIL

BIRTHDAY, ANNIVERSARY ETC

NAME

ADDRESS

HOME

MOBILE

WORK / FAX

E-MAIL

BIRTHDAY, ANNIVERSARY ETC

NAME

Address

Home

Mobile

Work / Fax

E-Mail

Birthday, Anniversary etc

NAME

Address

Home

Mobile

Work / Fax

E-Mail

Birthday, Anniversary etc

NAME

Address

Home

Mobile

Work / Fax

E-Mail

Birthday, Anniversary etc

NAME

ADDRESS

HOME

MOBILE

WORK / FAX

E-MAIL

BIRTHDAY, ANNIVERSARY ETC

NAME

ADDRESS

HOME

MOBILE

WORK / FAX

E-MAIL

BIRTHDAY, ANNIVERSARY ETC

NAME

ADDRESS

HOME

MOBILE

WORK / FAX

E-MAIL

BIRTHDAY, ANNIVERSARY ETC

NAME

ADDRESS

HOME

MOBILE

WORK / FAX

E-MAIL

BIRTHDAY, ANNIVERSARY ETC

NAME

ADDRESS

HOME

MOBILE

WORK / FAX

E-MAIL

BIRTHDAY, ANNIVERSARY ETC

NAME

ADDRESS

HOME

MOBILE

WORK / FAX

E-MAIL

BIRTHDAY, ANNIVERSARY ETC

NAME

ADDRESS

HOME

MOBILE

WORK / FAX

E-MAIL

BIRTHDAY, ANNIVERSARY ETC

NAME

ADDRESS

HOME

MOBILE

WORK / FAX

E-MAIL

BIRTHDAY, ANNIVERSARY ETC

NAME

ADDRESS

HOME

MOBILE

WORK / FAX

E-MAIL

BIRTHDAY, ANNIVERSARY ETC

NAME

ADDRESS

HOME

MOBILE

WORK / FAX

E-MAIL

BIRTHDAY, ANNIVERSARY ETC

NAME

ADDRESS

HOME

MOBILE

WORK / FAX

E-MAIL

BIRTHDAY, ANNIVERSARY ETC

NAME

ADDRESS

HOME

MOBILE

WORK / FAX

E-MAIL

BIRTHDAY, ANNIVERSARY ETC

NAME

ADDRESS

HOME

MOBILE

WORK / FAX

E-MAIL

BIRTHDAY, ANNIVERSARY ETC

NAME

ADDRESS

HOME

MOBILE

WORK / FAX

E-MAIL

BIRTHDAY, ANNIVERSARY ETC

NAME

ADDRESS

HOME

MOBILE

WORK / FAX

E-MAIL

BIRTHDAY, ANNIVERSARY ETC

NAME

ADDRESS

HOME

MOBILE

WORK / FAX

E-MAIL

BIRTHDAY, ANNIVERSARY ETC

NAME

ADDRESS

HOME

MOBILE

WORK / FAX

E-MAIL

BIRTHDAY, ANNIVERSARY ETC

NAME

ADDRESS

HOME

MOBILE

WORK / FAX

E-MAIL

BIRTHDAY, ANNIVERSARY ETC

NAME

ADDRESS

HOME

MOBILE

WORK / FAX

E-MAIL

BIRTHDAY, ANNIVERSARY ETC

NAME

ADDRESS

HOME

MOBILE

WORK / FAX

E-MAIL

BIRTHDAY, ANNIVERSARY ETC

NAME

ADDRESS

HOME

MOBILE

WORK / FAX

E-MAIL

BIRTHDAY, ANNIVERSARY ETC

NAME

ADDRESS

HOME

MOBILE

WORK / FAX

E-MAIL

BIRTHDAY, ANNIVERSARY ETC

NAME

ADDRESS

HOME

MOBILE

WORK / FAX

E-MAIL

BIRTHDAY, ANNIVERSARY ETC

NAME

ADDRESS

HOME

MOBILE

WORK / FAX

E-MAIL

BIRTHDAY, ANNIVERSARY ETC

NAME

ADDRESS

HOME

MOBILE

WORK / FAX

E-MAIL

BIRTHDAY, ANNIVERSARY ETC

NAME

ADDRESS

HOME

MOBILE

WORK / FAX

E-MAIL

BIRTHDAY, ANNIVERSARY ETC

NAME

ADDRESS

HOME

MOBILE

WORK / FAX

E-MAIL

BIRTHDAY, ANNIVERSARY ETC

NAME

ADDRESS

HOME

MOBILE

WORK / FAX

E-MAIL

BIRTHDAY, ANNIVERSARY ETC

NAME

ADDRESS

HOME

MOBILE

WORK / FAX

E-MAIL

BIRTHDAY, ANNIVERSARY ETC

NAME

ADDRESS

HOME

MOBILE

WORK / FAX

E-MAIL

BIRTHDAY, ANNIVERSARY ETC

NAME

ADDRESS

HOME

MOBILE

WORK / FAX

E-MAIL

BIRTHDAY, ANNIVERSARY ETC

NAME

ADDRESS

HOME

MOBILE

WORK / FAX

E-MAIL

BIRTHDAY, ANNIVERSARY ETC

NAME

ADDRESS

HOME

MOBILE

WORK / FAX

E-MAIL

BIRTHDAY, ANNIVERSARY ETC

NAME

ADDRESS

HOME

MOBILE

WORK / FAX

E-MAIL

BIRTHDAY, ANNIVERSARY ETC

NAME

ADDRESS

HOME

MOBILE

WORK / FAX

E-MAIL

BIRTHDAY, ANNIVERSARY ETC

NAME

ADDRESS

HOME

MOBILE

WORK / FAX

E-MAIL

BIRTHDAY, ANNIVERSARY ETC

NAME

ADDRESS

HOME

MOBILE

WORK / FAX

E-MAIL

BIRTHDAY, ANNIVERSARY ETC

NAME

ADDRESS

HOME

MOBILE

WORK / FAX

E-MAIL

BIRTHDAY, ANNIVERSARY ETC

NAME

ADDRESS

HOME

MOBILE

WORK / FAX

E-MAIL

BIRTHDAY, ANNIVERSARY ETC

NAME

ADDRESS

HOME

MOBILE

WORK / FAX

E-MAIL

BIRTHDAY, ANNIVERSARY ETC

NAME

ADDRESS

HOME

MOBILE

WORK / FAX

E-MAIL

BIRTHDAY, ANNIVERSARY ETC

NAME

ADDRESS

HOME

MOBILE

WORK / FAX

E-MAIL

BIRTHDAY, ANNIVERSARY ETC

NAME

ADDRESS

HOME

MOBILE

WORK / FAX

E-MAIL

BIRTHDAY, ANNIVERSARY ETC

NAME

ADDRESS

HOME

MOBILE

WORK / FAX

E-MAIL

BIRTHDAY, ANNIVERSARY ETC

NAME

ADDRESS

HOME

MOBILE

WORK / FAX

E-MAIL

BIRTHDAY, ANNIVERSARY ETC

NAME

ADDRESS

HOME

MOBILE

WORK / FAX

E-MAIL

BIRTHDAY, ANNIVERSARY ETC

NAME

ADDRESS

HOME

MOBILE

WORK / FAX

E-MAIL

BIRTHDAY, ANNIVERSARY ETC

NAME

ADDRESS

HOME

MOBILE

WORK / FAX

E-MAIL

BIRTHDAY, ANNIVERSARY ETC

NAME

Address

Home

Mobile

Work / Fax

E-Mail

Birthday, Anniversary etc

NAME

Address

Home

Mobile

Work / Fax

E-Mail

Birthday, Anniversary etc

NAME

Address

Home

Mobile

Work / Fax

E-Mail

Birthday, Anniversary etc

NAME

ADDRESS

HOME

MOBILE

WORK / FAX

E-MAIL

BIRTHDAY, ANNIVERSARY ETC

NAME

ADDRESS

HOME

MOBILE

WORK / FAX

E-MAIL

BIRTHDAY, ANNIVERSARY ETC

NAME

ADDRESS

HOME

MOBILE

WORK / FAX

E-MAIL

BIRTHDAY, ANNIVERSARY ETC

NAME

ADDRESS

HOME

MOBILE

WORK / FAX

E-MAIL

BIRTHDAY, ANNIVERSARY ETC

NAME

ADDRESS

HOME

MOBILE

WORK / FAX

E-MAIL

BIRTHDAY, ANNIVERSARY ETC

NAME

ADDRESS

HOME

MOBILE

WORK / FAX

E-MAIL

BIRTHDAY, ANNIVERSARY ETC

NAME

ADDRESS

HOME

MOBILE

WORK / FAX

E-MAIL

BIRTHDAY, ANNIVERSARY ETC

NAME

ADDRESS

HOME

MOBILE

WORK / FAX

E-MAIL

BIRTHDAY, ANNIVERSARY ETC

NAME

ADDRESS

HOME

MOBILE

WORK / FAX

E-MAIL

BIRTHDAY, ANNIVERSARY ETC

NAME

ADDRESS

HOME

MOBILE

WORK / FAX

E-MAIL

BIRTHDAY, ANNIVERSARY ETC

NAME

ADDRESS

HOME

MOBILE

WORK / FAX

E-MAIL

BIRTHDAY, ANNIVERSARY ETC

NAME

ADDRESS

HOME

MOBILE

WORK / FAX

E-MAIL

BIRTHDAY, ANNIVERSARY ETC

NAME

ADDRESS

HOME

MOBILE

WORK / FAX

E-MAIL

BIRTHDAY, ANNIVERSARY ETC

NAME

ADDRESS

HOME

MOBILE

WORK / FAX

E-MAIL

BIRTHDAY, ANNIVERSARY ETC

NAME

ADDRESS

HOME

MOBILE

WORK / FAX

E-MAIL

BIRTHDAY, ANNIVERSARY ETC

NAME

ADDRESS

HOME

MOBILE

WORK / FAX

E-MAIL

BIRTHDAY, ANNIVERSARY ETC

NAME

ADDRESS

HOME

MOBILE

WORK / FAX

E-MAIL

BIRTHDAY, ANNIVERSARY ETC

NAME

ADDRESS

HOME

MOBILE

WORK / FAX

E-MAIL

BIRTHDAY, ANNIVERSARY ETC

NAME

Address

Home

Mobile

Work / Fax

E-Mail

Birthday, Anniversary etc

NAME

Address

Home

Mobile

Work / Fax

E-Mail

Birthday, Anniversary etc

NAME

Address

Home

Mobile

Work / Fax

E-Mail

Birthday, Anniversary etc

NAME

Address

Home

Mobile

Work / Fax

E-Mail

Birthday, Anniversary etc

NAME

Address

Home

Mobile

Work / Fax

E-Mail

Birthday, Anniversary etc

NAME

Address

Home

Mobile

Work / Fax

E-Mail

Birthday, Anniversary etc

NAME

ADDRESS

HOME

MOBILE

WORK / FAX

E-MAIL

BIRTHDAY, ANNIVERSARY ETC

NAME

ADDRESS

HOME

MOBILE

WORK / FAX

E-MAIL

BIRTHDAY, ANNIVERSARY ETC

NAME

ADDRESS

HOME

MOBILE

WORK / FAX

E-MAIL

BIRTHDAY, ANNIVERSARY ETC

NAME

ADDRESS

HOME

MOBILE

WORK / FAX

E-MAIL

BIRTHDAY, ANNIVERSARY ETC

NAME

ADDRESS

HOME

MOBILE

WORK / FAX

E-MAIL

BIRTHDAY, ANNIVERSARY ETC

NAME

ADDRESS

HOME

MOBILE

WORK / FAX

E-MAIL

BIRTHDAY, ANNIVERSARY ETC

NAME

ADDRESS

HOME

MOBILE

WORK / FAX

E-MAIL

BIRTHDAY, ANNIVERSARY ETC

NAME

ADDRESS

HOME

MOBILE

WORK / FAX

E-MAIL

BIRTHDAY, ANNIVERSARY ETC

NAME

ADDRESS

HOME

MOBILE

WORK / FAX

E-MAIL

BIRTHDAY, ANNIVERSARY ETC

NAME

ADDRESS

HOME

MOBILE

WORK / FAX

E-MAIL

BIRTHDAY, ANNIVERSARY ETC

NAME

ADDRESS

HOME

MOBILE

WORK / FAX

E-MAIL

BIRTHDAY, ANNIVERSARY ETC

NAME

ADDRESS

HOME

MOBILE

WORK / FAX

E-MAIL

BIRTHDAY, ANNIVERSARY ETC

NAME

ADDRESS

HOME

MOBILE

WORK / FAX

E-MAIL

BIRTHDAY, ANNIVERSARY ETC

NAME

ADDRESS

HOME

MOBILE

WORK / FAX

E-MAIL

BIRTHDAY, ANNIVERSARY ETC

NAME

ADDRESS

HOME

MOBILE

WORK / FAX

E-MAIL

BIRTHDAY, ANNIVERSARY ETC

NAME

Address

Home

Mobile

Work / Fax

E-Mail

Birthday, Anniversary etc

NAME

Address

Home

Mobile

Work / Fax

E-Mail

Birthday, Anniversary etc

NAME

Address

Home

Mobile

Work / Fax

E-Mail

Birthday, Anniversary etc

NAME

ADDRESS

HOME

MOBILE

WORK / FAX

E-MAIL

BIRTHDAY, ANNIVERSARY ETC

NAME

ADDRESS

HOME

MOBILE

WORK / FAX

E-MAIL

BIRTHDAY, ANNIVERSARY ETC

NAME

ADDRESS

HOME

MOBILE

WORK / FAX

E-MAIL

BIRTHDAY, ANNIVERSARY ETC

NAME

ADDRESS

HOME

MOBILE

WORK / FAX

E-MAIL

BIRTHDAY, ANNIVERSARY ETC

NAME

ADDRESS

HOME

MOBILE

WORK / FAX

E-MAIL

BIRTHDAY, ANNIVERSARY ETC

NAME

ADDRESS

HOME

MOBILE

WORK / FAX

E-MAIL

BIRTHDAY, ANNIVERSARY ETC

NAME

ADDRESS

HOME

MOBILE

WORK / FAX

E-MAIL

BIRTHDAY, ANNIVERSARY ETC

NAME

ADDRESS

HOME

MOBILE

WORK / FAX

E-MAIL

BIRTHDAY, ANNIVERSARY ETC

NAME

ADDRESS

HOME

MOBILE

WORK / FAX

E-MAIL

BIRTHDAY, ANNIVERSARY ETC

NAME

ADDRESS

HOME

MOBILE

WORK / FAX

E-MAIL

BIRTHDAY, ANNIVERSARY ETC

NAME

ADDRESS

HOME

MOBILE

WORK / FAX

E-MAIL

BIRTHDAY, ANNIVERSARY ETC

NAME

ADDRESS

HOME

MOBILE

WORK / FAX

E-MAIL

BIRTHDAY, ANNIVERSARY ETC

NAME

ADDRESS

HOME

MOBILE

WORK / FAX

E-MAIL

BIRTHDAY, ANNIVERSARY ETC

NAME

ADDRESS

HOME

MOBILE

WORK / FAX

E-MAIL

BIRTHDAY, ANNIVERSARY ETC

NAME

ADDRESS

HOME

MOBILE

WORK / FAX

E-MAIL

BIRTHDAY, ANNIVERSARY ETC

NAME

ADDRESS

HOME

MOBILE

WORK / FAX

E-MAIL

BIRTHDAY, ANNIVERSARY ETC

NAME

ADDRESS

HOME

MOBILE

WORK / FAX

E-MAIL

BIRTHDAY, ANNIVERSARY ETC

NAME

ADDRESS

HOME

MOBILE

WORK / FAX

E-MAIL

BIRTHDAY, ANNIVERSARY ETC

NAME

ADDRESS

HOME

MOBILE

WORK / FAX

E-MAIL

BIRTHDAY, ANNIVERSARY ETC

NAME

ADDRESS

HOME

MOBILE

WORK / FAX

E-MAIL

BIRTHDAY, ANNIVERSARY ETC

NAME

ADDRESS

HOME

MOBILE

WORK / FAX

E-MAIL

BIRTHDAY, ANNIVERSARY ETC

NAME

Address

Home

Mobile

Work / Fax

E-Mail

Birthday, Anniversary etc

NAME

Address

Home

Mobile

Work / Fax

E-Mail

Birthday, Anniversary etc

NAME

Address

Home

Mobile

Work / Fax

E-Mail

Birthday, Anniversary etc

NAME

ADDRESS

HOME

MOBILE

WORK / FAX

E-MAIL

BIRTHDAY, ANNIVERSARY ETC

NAME

ADDRESS

HOME

MOBILE

WORK / FAX

E-MAIL

BIRTHDAY, ANNIVERSARY ETC

NAME

ADDRESS

HOME

MOBILE

WORK / FAX

E-MAIL

BIRTHDAY, ANNIVERSARY ETC

NAME

ADDRESS

HOME

MOBILE

WORK / FAX

E-MAIL

BIRTHDAY, ANNIVERSARY ETC

NAME

ADDRESS

HOME

MOBILE

WORK / FAX

E-MAIL

BIRTHDAY, ANNIVERSARY ETC

NAME

ADDRESS

HOME

MOBILE

WORK / FAX

E-MAIL

BIRTHDAY, ANNIVERSARY ETC

NAME

ADDRESS

HOME

MOBILE

WORK / FAX

E-MAIL

BIRTHDAY, ANNIVERSARY ETC

NAME

ADDRESS

HOME

MOBILE

WORK / FAX

E-MAIL

BIRTHDAY, ANNIVERSARY ETC

NAME

ADDRESS

HOME

MOBILE

WORK / FAX

E-MAIL

BIRTHDAY, ANNIVERSARY ETC

NAME

ADDRESS

HOME

MOBILE

WORK / FAX

E-MAIL

BIRTHDAY, ANNIVERSARY ETC

NAME

ADDRESS

HOME

MOBILE

WORK / FAX

E-MAIL

BIRTHDAY, ANNIVERSARY ETC

NAME

ADDRESS

HOME

MOBILE

WORK / FAX

E-MAIL

BIRTHDAY, ANNIVERSARY ETC

NAME

ADDRESS

HOME

MOBILE

WORK / FAX

E-MAIL

BIRTHDAY, ANNIVERSARY ETC

NAME

ADDRESS

HOME

MOBILE

WORK / FAX

E-MAIL

BIRTHDAY, ANNIVERSARY ETC

NAME

ADDRESS

HOME

MOBILE

WORK / FAX

E-MAIL

BIRTHDAY, ANNIVERSARY ETC

19359184R00072

Printed in Great Britain
by Amazon